IMAGES OF SINGAPORE

PHOTOS BY BERNARD GO

Marshall Cavendish
Editions

© 2016 Marshall Cavendish International (Asia) Private Limited

Concept & Series Editor: Melvin Neo
Design & Photographs: Bernard Go Kwang Meng

Published 2011, reprinted 2012; 2nd edition published 2013, reprinted (twice); 3rd edition published
2014, reprinted 2015. This 4th edition published in 2016, reprinted 2018 by Marshall Cavendish Editions
An imprint of Marshall Cavendish International

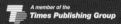

A member of the
Times Publishing Group

Other Marshall Cavendish Offices:
Marshall Cavendish Corporation. 99 White Plains Road, Tarrytown NY 10591-9001, USA • Marshall
Cavendish International (Thailand) Co Ltd. 253 Asoke, 12th Flr, Sukhumvit 21 Road, Klongtoey Nua,
Wattana, Bangkok 10110, Thailand • Marshall Cavendish (Malaysia) Sdn Bhd, Times Subang, Lot 46,
Subang Hi-Tech Industrial Park, Batu Tiga, 40000 Shah Alam, Selangor Darul Ehsan, Malaysia.

Marshall Cavendish is a registered trademark of Times Publishing Limited

National Library Board, Singapore Cataloguing-in-Publication Data
Name(s): Go, Bernard Kwang Meng, photographer.
Title: Images of Singapore / photos by Bernard Go.
Description: Singapore : Marshall Cavendish Editions, 2016. Previous edition published 2014.
Identifier(s): OCN 953683522 | ISBN 978-981-4751-23-0 (paperback)
Subject(s): LCSH: Singapore--Pictorial works | Singapore--Social life and customs-- Pictorial works.
Classification: DDC 959.57--dc23

Printed in Singapore

On the cover: View of Christmas light-up at the Gardens by the Bay.

All photos by Bernard Go except as indicated: Capella Singapore pg 55; Edward Hendricks pg 27
(top right and bottom right); Katong Antique House pg 27 (left); Marina Bay Sands Pte Ltd pg 153

IMAGES OF SINGAPORE

CONTENTS

01 INTRODUCTION

Singapore started life as a small fishing village and later became a key trading port in Southeast Asia. Today, the country is a unique blend of modernity and tradition and has one of the world's fastest rates of economic growth.

Military displays by the Singapore Armed Forces are a perennial parade highlight.

NATIONAL DAY

A fomer British colony, Singapore later became part of the Federation of Malaysia before it officially gained independence on 9 August 1965. The momentous occasion is commemorated annually with an exciting National Day Parade.

NATIONAL FLOWER

The Vanda Miss Joachim was chosen as Singapore's national flower in 1981. The lovely purple orchid was selected for its hardy resilient qualities and ability to bloom throughout the year.

NATIONAL FLAG

The national flag of Singapore was first adopted in 1965. It comprises two equal horizontal sections of red (on top) and white (below); red representing universal brotherhood while white symbolises everlasting purity and virtue. The white crescent moon represents a young nation, and the five stars symbolise the nation's ideals: democracy, peace, progress, justice and equality.

A multicultural mix of immigrants from around the region, Singapore society comprises three main ethnic groups — Chinese, Malays, Indians — with other smaller ethnic groups such as the Peranakans and Eurasians. Each community's rich heritage and cultural values are deeply ingrained into the fabric of Singapore's past and present.

02

PEOPLE & CULTURE

CHINESE

Ethnic Chinese make up almost three-quarters of the
population in Singapore. They come from dialect groups.
such as Hokkien, Cantonese, Teochew and Hakka.
Each group has its own language, although most speak
Mandarin as a common platform for conversation.

CHINESE NEW YEAR

Chinese New Year is one of the most celebrated festivals
in the Chinese calendar. Extended families gather
on the eve of Chinese New Year for a reunion dinner.
Traditionally, red packets (or *hong bao*) containing money
are given to younger members of the family for good luck.

The festivities are concentrated in Chinatown, where
the streets are decorated in red (signifying good luck),
and the smells of *bak kwa* (barbecued pork) and other
traditional snacks and Chinese New Year tunes fill the air.
Spicing up the festivities during this 15-day celebration are
the River Hong Bao Carnival and Chingay Parade.

CHINGAY PARADE

This street parade was first held in 1973 as part of the Lunar New Year celebrations. It proved to be very popular and has since become an annual event. Over the years, the Chingay Parade has gone multicultural and even international with performers coming from all over the world. Today it is the largest street performance and float parade in Asia.

MID-AUTUMN FESTIVAL

Also known as the Mooncake or Lantern Festival, the Mid-Autumn Festival usually falls in August as it follows the Chinese lunar calendar. Families and friends give one another mooncakes, which are delicious pastries filled with ingredients such as lotus paste, red bean and salted egg yolk. Chinatown is a swirl of activity and its streets are beautifully lit with dazzling lantern displays. Events such as lantern installations and special performances are also organised all over Singapore in celebration of this festival.

MALAY

The Malays are the second largest ethnic group in Singapore. This warm and hospitable community traces its ancestry to the Bugis from Sulawesi, the Boyanese from Madura in Indonesia and the Orang Laut, who are descendants of the Sea Gypsies.

HARI RAYA PUASA

Hari Raya Puasa is celebrated after the Islamic fasting month of Ramadan. During Hari Raya Puasa, Muslims dress in traditional ethnic clothing, children receive money in green packets (*duit raya*) and younger Muslims seek forgiveness from their elders for any misdeeds.

The districts of Geylang Serai and Kampong Glam are abuzz with street performances and light-ups. There are also numerous bazaars all over the island selling delectable Malay snacks and treats.

INDIAN

The smallest of the three major ethnic groups, the Indians were originally immigrants who arrived in Singapore to work and provide for their families back home. Over time, they brought their families with them and settled down permanently. The community is a tight-knit one, and still practices many traditions and customs from the Indian subcontinent.

DEEPAVALI

Deepavali is also known as the Festival of Lights and celebrates Lord Krishna's victory over the demon of darkness. Hindus commemorate the triumph of good over evil by lighting oil lamps. They also wear new clothes to mark the occasion and family and friends visit one another.

Little India in the Serangoon area is an explosion of the senses during Deepavali. Shops selling garlands, oil lamps and gorgeous saris line the streets alongside stalls hawking all sorts of delicious food. Festive lights adorn the roads and trees, adding to the electrifying atmosphere.

Each Deepavali, the streets of Little India come alive in a spectacular display of festive lights.

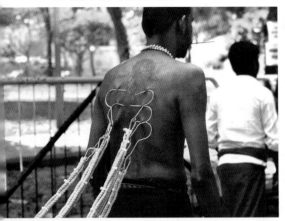

THAIPUSAM

One of the most amazing festivals in Singapore, Thaipusam is not for the faint hearted. In a show of devotion and gratitude to Lord Murugan, devotees carry a *kavadi*, a heavy steel framework that is anchored to their bare bodies. Devotees also pierce their tongue, cheeks, lips and other body parts with skewers, spikes and other similar sharp objects. They then walk barefoot for about 4 km. Other believers join in the procession, carrying milk jars in offering to Lord Murugan.

PERANAKAN

Many of the early Chinese immigrants to Malaya and married Malay women, giving birth to a community of people known as the Peranakans (which means "locally born"). Also known as Straits Chinese or Straits-born Chinese, the Peranakans pride themselves on their unique culture and cuisine, which has evolved and developed over the centuries. The Katong area has traditionally been a Peranakan enclave, featuring shophouses with elaborate facades and decorative tiles.

03

ARCHITECTURAL ICONS

Gleaming, modern skyscrapers sit beside charming colonial-era buildings and busy wet markets in Singapore — a dynamic architectural mix of old and new, East and West, and past and present.

ISTANA

Designed in the neo-Palladian style from the 18th century, the Istana is Singapore's equivalent of the White House and the official residence of the president of Singapore. Originally built in 1867 as the home of Singapore's first colonial governor, the Istana — which means "palace" in Malay — is where the president receives and entertains state guests.

STAMFORD RAFFLES STATUE

A bronze statue of Sir Stamford Raffles was installed in 1887 at the Padang. It was moved to the front of the Victoria Theatre and Concert Hall at Empress Place in 1919. A white marble replica of that statue (shown here) was later placed at the mouth of the Singapore River, marking Raffles' landing site on the island in 1819.

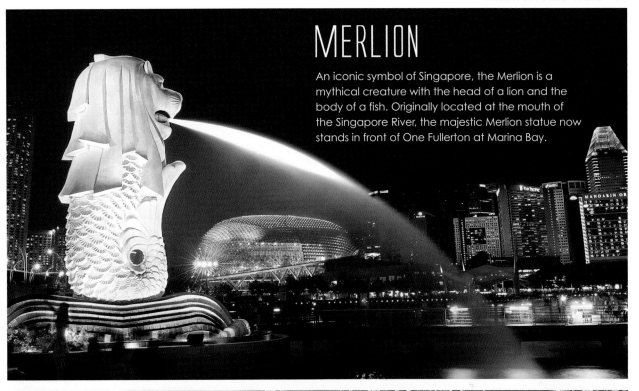

MERLION

An iconic symbol of Singapore, the Merlion is a mythical creature with the head of a lion and the body of a fish. Originally located at the mouth of the Singapore River, the majestic Merlion statue now stands in front of One Fullerton at Marina Bay.

RAFFLES HOTEL

Named after Sir Stamford Raffles, the founder of Singapore, the Raffles Hotel is a luxurious colonial-style hotel dating back to 1887. An oasis of lush tropical gardens in the heart of the city, the hotel is renowned for its elegant French Renaissance architecture and impeccable service.

RAFFLES HOTEL

The world's largest kinetic art sculpture; Kinetic Rain comprising 1,216 bronze droplets, moves to a specially choreographed dance every day.

CHANGI AIRPORT

Since Changi Airport opened in 1981, it has won more than 450 accolades including world's best airport from organisations around the world. One of the world's busiest international airports, Changi handles more than 55.4 million pasengers annually. Today, the three passenger terminals serve more than 100 airlines flying to over 320 cities in 80 countries and territories worldwide.

THE ARTS HOUSE

Singapore's former Parliament House is a grand Victorian-style structure. It was designed and built by colonial architect, George Coleman in 1827. The building was converted into an arts and heritage venue in 2004 and relaunched as The Arts House. Today, it is a popular venue for the Arts and hosts book launches, films, art exhibitions, plays and musical concerts. Taking pride of place outside the building is a majestic bronze elephant, a gift from King Rama V of Thailand in 1871.

THE FULLERTON HOTEL

Built in 1928 and named after Robert Fullerton who was the first Governor of the Straits Settlements, the Fullerton Building used to house the General Post Office, the Chamber of Commerce and The Singapore Club. Once an important trade and economic centre, this magnificent colonial building is now the luxurious Fullerton Hotel overlooking the Singapore River.

ESPLANADE THEATRES ON THE BAY

Singapore's epicentre of the arts, the Esplanade is one of the world's busiest performing arts centres — home to a grand concert hall, outdoor theatre, recital and theatre studio, as well as numerous restaurants and specialty cafes and even a public library.

Strategically located by the Marina Bay waterfront, the Esplanade is dubbed the "durian" because of its unique louvered roof, which bears a resemblance to the pungent, thorny fruit of the Southeast Asian region.

The 220-metre long Jubilee Bridge was opened in March 2015. It links the Esplanade promenade with the Merlion Park located across the Singapore River.

ESPLANADE: PERFORMING ARTS FOR EVERYONE

"It is a name (esplanade) beloved of all Singaporeans, for it conjures in the mind respite from the day's exertions, tropical sea breezes, the aroma of satay, glittering harbour lights, romance beneath the stars."

George Yeo
Minister for Information and the Arts (1994)

SRI MARIAMMAN TEMPLE

Singapore's oldest Hindu temple, the Sri Mariamman Temple, is rather surprisingly located in the heart of Chinatown. The landmark temple has tiers of various gods and deities from Hindu mythology carved on its main structure, and remains a key focal point of the Indian community.

SULTAN MOSQUE

Originally built between 1824 and 1926 by Sultan Hussain Shah, the first sultan of Singapore, the Sultan Mosque is a regal arabesque structure replete with domes, minarets and balustrades. The mosque has gone through many stages of development and today has a prayer hall which can accommodate up to 5,000 people in mass prayer. The Sultan Mosque is a gazetted national monument.

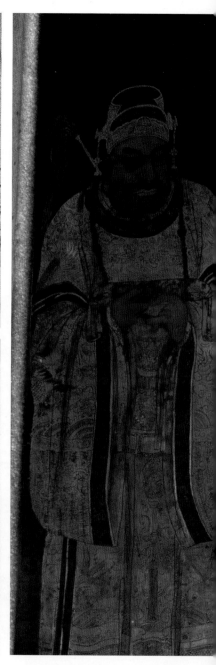

THIAN HOCK KENG TEMPLE

Built on the site of a popular joss house at Telok Ayer Street, the Thian Hock Keng Temple is one of Singapore's oldest Chinese temples. The richly-ornamented building has curved roofs and sharp edges decorated with animals from mythical Chinese folklore. Following a major restoration, the landmark temple was awarded the UNESCO Asia-Pacific Heritage Conservation Award in 2001.

ST. ANDREW'S CATHEDRAL

Singapore's first and largest Anglican Church was built in 1857 by Colonel Ronald MacPherson of the Madras army. With its extended pinnacles, arched entrance and glossy white exterior, the majestic building was gazetted as a national monument in 1973, and is one of Singapore's most treasured works of architecture.

GOODWOOD PARK HOTEL

Built in 1900, the former Teutonia Club served the German expatriate community in Singapore during its colonial years. The building features ornamental works and a large semi-circular gable end flanking the entrance. Today it is the Goodwood Park Hotel. It was declared a national monument in 1989.

CAPELLA SINGAPORE

This five-star hotel on Sentosa Island sits on over 30 acres of lush rainforest with views of the South China Sea. Two colonial buildings built in the 1880s by the British Military form the heart of the luxurious resort. These have been carefully restored and integrated with new buildings and sculpture gardens filled with contemporary art.

PUBLIC HOUSING

Many Singaporeans live in high-rise HDB (Housing Development Board) flats, which are located in public housing estates with amenities such as hawker centres, shops, medical clinics and recreational facilities within walking distance.

The nation's progressive economic development is reflected in the changing face of its public housing, from the low structures of yesteryear to the gleaming blocks of today.

CHIJMES

Formerly a Catholic girls school and convent (Convent of the Holy Infant Jesus) in the mid-19th century, CHIJMES was the seat of education for generations of Singapore girls until the school relocated in 1983. The neo-Gothic style building has since been restored and is now a popular retail, dining and entertainment venue.

EST. 1841

CHIJMES

VICTORIA THEATRE & CONCERT HALL

The complex comprises two buildings and a clock tower joined by a common corridor. The first hall was completed in 1862 and with the second hall and clock tower added in the early 1990s in memory of Queen Victoria who died in 1901. The Victoria Theatre and Concert Hall has undergone a number of renovations and refurbishment over the years with the most recent completed in 2014.

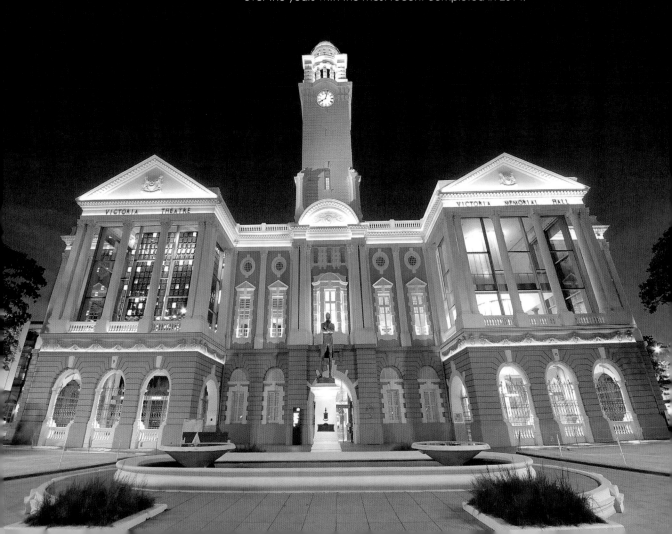

ASIAN CIVILIZATIONS MUSEUM

Erected in 1867, the Empress Place Building located beside the Singapore River housed colonial and Singapore government offices for over 100 years. It reopened as the Asian Civilisations Museum in 2003 after extensive conservation and renovation. The Museum seeks to promote a better understanding of the country's rich ethnic heritage.

NATIONAL GALLERY

Housed in the former Supreme Court and City Hall, the National Gallery Singapore is the country's newest art institution and was officially opened in November 2015. The Gallery oversees the largest public collection of modern art in Southeast Asia.

CAPITOL SINGAPORE

The historic Capitol Theatre was built in 1933 by the architectural firm Keys & Dowdeswell. After the Second World War, it operated as a cinema under Shaw Organisation for 40-odd years until it was acquired by the Urban Redevelopment Authority in 1987. Today it is part of Capitol Singapore, a mixed-use development comprising shops, restaurants, a theatre/cinema, apartments and a luxury hotel.

PARKROYAL ON PICKERING

Located on the fringe of the Central Business District facing Hong Lim Park, Parkroyal on Pickering is a striking landmark in the city with its unusual landscaped podium block. The hotel designed by WOHA Architects has won numerous international accolades for its architecural design and the innovative use of new construction methods and materials in order to be friendly to the environment.

NATIONAL STADIUM

The National Stadium is part of the multi-purpose Singapore Sports Hub opened in 2014. The Stadium features the world's largest dome structure and a retractable roof. It has been custom-designed to host football, rugby, cricket and athletics events. Automated retractable seating also allows the space to be configured for concerts and entertainment programmes. The Sports Hub includes an aquatic centre, a multi-purpose arena, an indoor stadium, the Singapore Sports Museum and a shopping mall.

04

LOCALES

From the ultramodern business district to authentic cultural enclaves bursting with exotic sights, scents and smells, the Little Red Dot is home to a diverse spectrum of exciting locales.

CENTRAL BUSINESS DISTRICT

The heart of Singapore's financial hub, the Central Business District includes core financial and commercial areas such as Marina Bay, Raffles Place and Shenton Way. Big international names jostle cheek to cheek with local ones in towering skyscrapers overlooking the Singapore River and the Marina Barrage.

LITTLE INDIA

Once the locale of the original Tamil migrants, Little India today bustles with traditional shophouses and colourful shops interspersed with temples. A treasure trove for the senses, the district offers everything from traditional fortune-telling and delicate saris to the heady scents of jasmine garlands, exotic spices and delicious Indian delicacies.

CHINATOWN

This area offers a fascinating peek into Singapore's rich Chinese culture and its history. Explore the beautifully-restored shophouses, family-run goldsmith shops and colourful textile stores. Food has a strong presence here. Dim sum restaurants and genteel teahouses line the lanes and alleyways, and Smith Street, an alfresco paradise of local delicacies, is a popular haunt for locals and visitors alike.

BUDDHA TOOTH RELIC TEMPLE & MUSEUM

This temple in the heart of Chinatown houses what Buddhist leaders regard as the Sacred Buddha Tooth Relic in a stupa made from 320 kg of gold donated by devotees. Founded by Venerable Shi Fa Zhao, the design of the temple is based on the elements and history of the Tang Dynasty and the Buddhist Mandala, the latter which is a representation of the Buddhist universe. Other highlights found in this complex include the Buddhist Culture Museum, Eminent Sangha Museum, Tripitaka Chamber, and a theatre for cultural performances, talks and films.

KAMPONG GLAM

Once the seat of the Malay royalty in Singapore, Kampong Glam has been an iconic Malay-Muslim precinct since the early 1800s. Awash with exotic smells, sights and sounds – from fragrant spices and traditional hand-woven carpets to modern art galleries and curios shops – its bustling alleyways are a treasure trove of art and culture to excite the senses.

At the heart of Kampong Glam's vibrancy is the Sultan Mosque, one of Singapore's most prominent national monuments. The site was designated a heritage conservation area in 1989.

GEYLANG SERAI

During the Muslim festive seasons, the Geylang Serai area comes to life in a riot of colours, with night markets and stalls selling everything from traditional attire to festive goodies and intricate handicrafts. The renovated Geylang Serai Market is filled with shops offering fresh produce and ethnic clothing and trinkets, as well as some of the best Malay and Indian-Muslim dishes in Singapore.

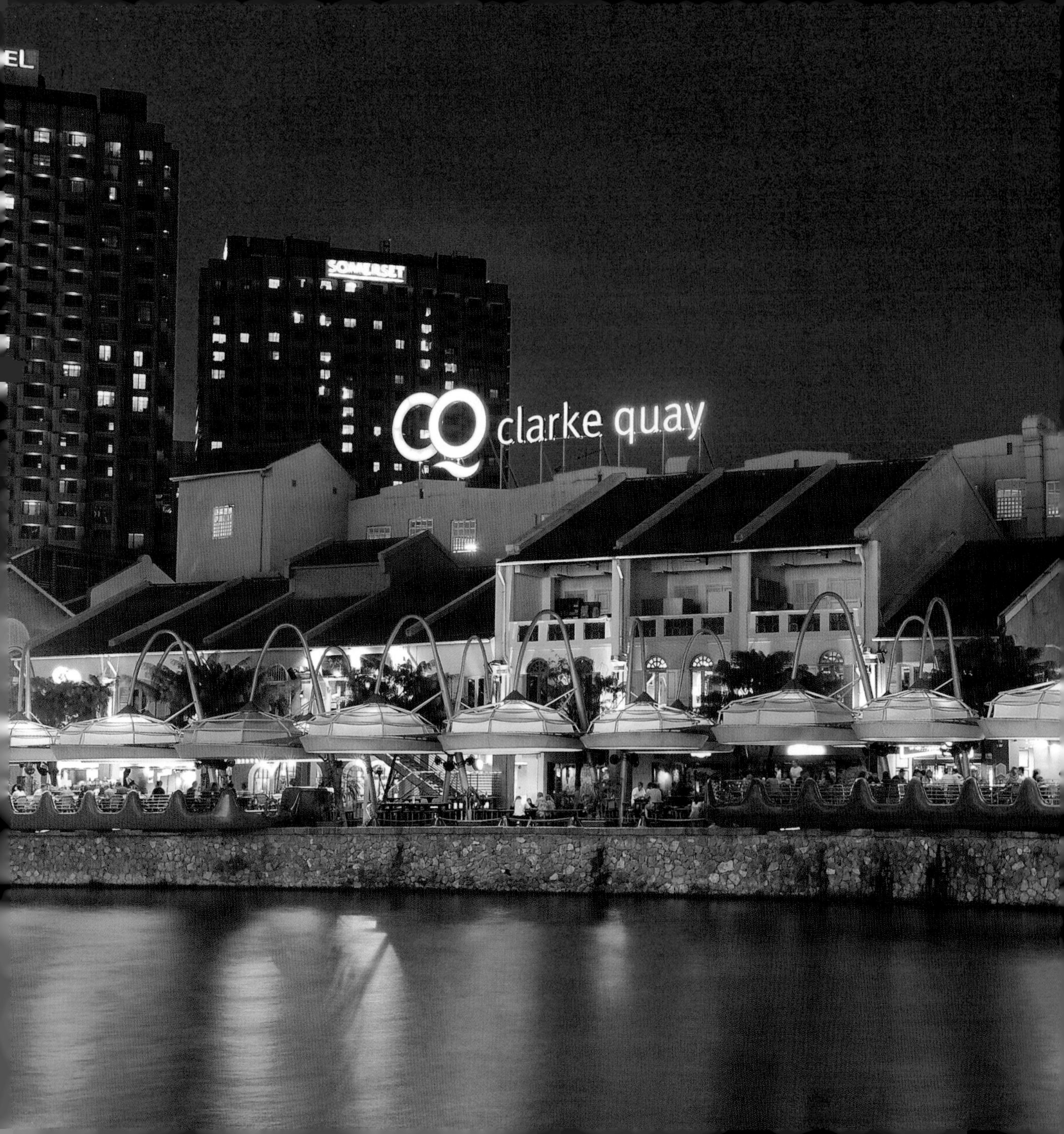
SOMERSET
clarke quay

CLARKE QUAY

A historical riverside quay situated at the mouth of the Singapore River, Clarke Quay was Singapore's epicentre of commerce in the late 19th century. Today, the bustling waterfront enclave pays homage to its heritage with a colourful kaleidoscope of restaurants, wine bars, entertainment spots and retail shops nestled amidst rows of charming shophouses, modern pushcarts and five-foot-way merchants.

ORCHARD ROAD

Deriving its name from the numerous fruit orchards and plantations that used to span the area, Singapore's famed Orchard Road is the equivalent of Los Angeles' Rodeo Drive or Tokyo's Omotesando. Testament to its reputation as a shopping haven, the premier shopping belt is lined cheek to cheek with high-end shopping malls and luxury hotels.

05

NATURE

Often celebrated as a cosmopolitan "Garden City",
Singapore's cityscape is complemented by its
thriving ecosystem of lush greenery, nature and
wildlife. From the trees and flora lining the island
to landscaped gardens and protected rainforests,
Singapore's numerous green enclaves offer close
commune with nature, even in the heart of the city.

BOTANIC GARDENS

Founded in 1859, the Singapore Botanic Gardens was given UNESCO World Heritage Site status in 2015. The Gardens encompass 64 hectares of verdant greenery and includes the National Orchid Garden with over 1,000 species and 2,000 hybrids of tropical orchids – the largest such display in the world.

Bathe in the urban oasis of the Singapore Botanic Gardens – from leisurely evening strolls to a relaxing picnic on the lawn, this green sanctuary is the perfect place to recharge and rejuvenate.

GARDENS BY THE BAY

This park in the heart of Singapore's city centre comprises three waterfront gardens: Bay South Garden, Bay East Garden and Bay Central Garden.

The Gardens includes two cooled conservatories – the Flower Dome and the Cloud Forest. The Flower Dome replicates cool dry conditions and features plants from the Mediterranean and semi-arid tropical regions. The Cloud Forest features the cool moist conditions found in tropical mountain regions.

A key feature are the 18 supertrees that dominate the Gardens' landscape. These supertrees are vertical gardens equipped with cells to harvest solar energy and also provide a framework for over 200 species and varieties of orchids, ferns and tropical flowering climbers. An elevated walkway linking two of the supertrees provides breathtaking aerial views of the Gardens.

SUNGEI BULOH WETLAND RESERVE

On the northwestern end of Singapore is a rare oasis, a thriving wetland of brackish and fresh-water ponds, mangrove mudflats, estuaries and swamps. Popular with nature and adventure enthusiasts, Sungei Buloh Wetland Reserve is home to a vast ecosystem of wildlife and lush flora and fauna, including kingfishers, mudskippers, otters and the rare Malayan water monitor.

MACRITCHIE RESERVOIR

One of Singapore's most popular nature parks, MacRitchie Reservoir is a protected water catchment reserve with over 3,000 hectares of surrounding rainforest. Boardwalks and rugged walking trails provide an instant escape from the concrete jungle of the city, and the HSBC Treetop Walk *(below)*, a 250-metre aerial suspension bridge that spans the two highest points in MacRitchie, offers a panoramic view of the rainforest canopy.

SOUTHERN RIDGES

Combining several walking trails through the hills of Mount Faber Park, Telok Blangah Hill Park and Kent Ridge Park, the Southern Ridges is home to many of Mother Nature's greatest gifts, and the purveyor of some of the most spectacular views of the city. Popular trails include the Canopy, Hilltop and Forest Walks, as well as the undulating Henderson Waves *(left)*, the highest pedestrian bridge in Singapore.

PULAU UBIN

Discover what life was like in 1960s Singapore on Pulau Ubin, a small island northeast of Singapore and home of the last *kampong* (village) from bygone days. Meaning "Granite Island" in Malay, the island was once known for its numerous granite quarries that supplied the local construction industry. Today, Pulau Ubin is a popular getaway destination for cyclists and nature lovers.

Main picture shows Chek Jawa, an intertidal flat and one-time coral reef on Pulau Ubin that boasts a virtually untouched sanctuary of rich ecosystems and marine wildlife.

CHINESE GARDEN

Built in 1975 and designed by a renowned Taiwanese architect, the serene Chinese Garden is modelled after the northern Chinese imperial style of integrating landscape and architecture. Enjoy a leisurely stroll amidst majestic pagodas, rainbow bridges and a gentle stream, and marvel at the beautiful Bonsai Garden, which features over a thousand bonsai trees from China.

BUKIT TIMAH NATURE RESERVE

Designated a protected reserve in 1883, Bukit Timah Nature Reserve
is the only substantial area of primary rainforest left in Singapore. The
163-hectare Reserve includes Bukit Timah Hill, Singapore's highest hill,
and is home to one of the world's most diverse ecological systems. In fact,
the number of tree species growing in a mere hectare of the Reserve is
more than the total number of tree species in all of North America.

EAST COAST PARK

The largest park in Singapore, East Coast Park is built entirely on reclaimed land with a man-made beach protected by breakwaters. Its cool sea breezes and myriad of available recreational activities makes the beachside park a popular weekend family destination, with chalets and barbecue pits, bicycle and inline skate rental, and even wakeboarding facilities all within walking distance.

06

FOOD

Singaporean food is as exotic and varied as its people. From delicious Chinese cuisine and spicy curries to wonderful breads and tasty nyonya goodies, the Republic's rich multicultural heritage offers a gourmet paradise that will appeal to even the most discerning tastebuds.

CHILLI CRAB

HAINANESE CHICKEN RICE

A dish best eaten using one's hands, chilli crab is a heady concoction of hard shell crabs seared in a rich, thick tomato, egg and chilli-based gravy. One of Singapore's favourite dishes, chilli crab is often eaten with *mantou*, delicious fried buns that help to soak up the remaining sauce.

Hainanese chicken rice is widely considered to be Singapore's national dish. Adapted to local tastes by Hainanese immigrants, the flavourful dish consists of fragrant rice cooked in chicken stock, slices of steamed chicken and cucumber and accompanied by chilli sauce, ginger paste and dark soy sauce.

SATAY

ROTI PRATA

Delicious skewers of marinated meat — usually chicken, beef or lamb — grilled over charcoal, satay is traditionally served with slivers of raw onions, chewy *ketupat* (rice cake) cubes, cucumber slices and a spicy peanut gravy.

A traditional Indian speciality, roti prata is a flaky flatbread pancake fried on a griddle to give it its golden-brown colour. Usually served with a spicy curry gravy, popular variants include roti prata with cheese, egg, mushrooms or even bananas and chocolate.

CHAR KWAY TEOW

POPIAH

Another of Singapore's signature dishes, char kway teow is a fried flat rice noodle dish, often tossed with prawns, egg, cockles, bean sprouts and sweet, dark sauce. The secret of a good char kway teow lies in the quality of ingredients and skill in achieving "*wok hei*", the smoky flavour from a hot wok.

A fresh spring roll made from a soft, paper-like crepe, traditional popiah is filled with a variety of ingredients such as steamed turnip, bean sprouts, omelette strips, cucumber, egg, chopped peanuts and shrimp, together with a sweet sauce.

LAKSA

FRIED CARROT CAKE

A popular Peranakan dish, laksa comprises thick rice noodles steeped in a spicy gravy thickened with aromatic spices, dried shrimp and coconut milk. The tasty dish is often topped with thinly sliced cucumber, bean sprouts, fresh cockles, prawns and fish cakes, as well as sambal chilli and finely chopped laksa leaves.

Often mistaken to be an actual 'cake', fried carrot cake in Singapore is in fact made from radish steamed with rice flour. The resulting 'cake' is then stir fried and mixed with preserved radish (chye poh), eggs, chilli, diced garlic and spring onion. There are two popular variants: "black" with caramelised sweet black sauce and "white" with just the crispy fried egg charred to golden perfection.

ROJAK

MEE SIAM

Rojak is a savoury fruit and vegetable salad made from a medley of ingredients, including cucumber, turnip, pineapple, bean sprouts, grilled cuttlefish, crushed peanuts and fried dough sticks (*you char kueh*) all tossed in a flavourful dressing. This sticky dark sauce contains tamarind sauce, prawn paste, chilli and sugar. The result is an exquisite combination of savoury, sweet and sour flavours that is both delicious and refreshing.

Mee siam is a Malay speciality made of thin rice noodles fried with prawn paste and spices. Served with dried bean curd (*tau pok*), boiled egg and paired with an aromatic, sweet and sour, salted soy bean gravy, this well-loved dish is garnished with Chinese chives.

KUEH PIE TEE

TANG YUAN

A classic nyonya favourite, kueh pie tee are dainty, crispy pastry cups filled with stewed turnip and shredded bamboo shoots, and topped with a variety of ingredients such as succulent prawns, egg strips, fresh parsley and chilli sauce.

Traditionally eaten during the 15th day of the Chinese New Year, tang yuan are glutinous rice balls cooked in a light ginger or peanut soup. Served plain or with delicious fillings such as red bean, peanut or sesame paste, the tang yuan's round shape symbolises family togetherness and as such, they are usually eaten together with one's family.

VADAI

PULUT HITAM

Vadai are a tasty South Indian snack made from ground lentils, dhal or diced potato, generously seasoned with onions, curry leaves, chilli and black mustard seeds. These deep-fried fritters are best eaten while still hot and crunchy, accompanied with coconut chutney and *sambar*, a vegetable stew based on a tamarind broth.

Usually eaten as a tea time treat, pulut hitam ('black rice' in Malay) is a sweet porridge made with black glutinous rice. This popular dessert is drizzled with fragrant coconut milk just before serving and sometimes topped with dried longan, a tropical fruit native to Southeast Asia.

DURIAN

SINGAPORE SLING

The pungent "king of fruits", as the durian is commonly known, is an acquired taste. The creamy golden flesh ensconced in a thorny husk has been described to taste like anything from a rich almond-flavoured custard to cream cheese and even the occasional wet rag. With its strong, distinctive odour, the durian is banned on all modes of public transport within Singapore.

The Singapore Sling is synonymous with the Raffles Hotel, where the popular cocktail is reputed to have been created in the early 1900s. A unique concoction containing gin, cherry brandy, pineapple juice, Cointreau and Grenadine, amongst others, the Singapore Sling is the main draw at the hotel's renowned Long Bar.

From the high-octane exhilaration of the world's first-ever Formula 1 night race to the majestic Integrated Resorts and Sentosa, Singapore's all-in-one entertainment and leisure hotspot, there's something for everyone from the young to the young-at-heart.

ATTRACTIONS

SENTOSA

Once a small fishing village just south of the main island of Singapore, Sentosa is today a bustling island resort. It is home to Resorts World Sentosa Integrated Resort and Southeast Asia's first Universal Studios theme park, as well as a range of attractions that include a dolphin lagoon and ZoukOut, the popular annual beachside dance festival.

RESORTS WORLD SENTOSA

One of the country's two Integrated Resorts, Resorts World Sentosa is a 49-hectare entertainment and leisure playground. Universal Studios Singapore, S.E.A. Aquarium, Adventure Cove, six world-class hotels, a grand casino and an eclectic array of celebrity chef restaurants and brand-name boutiques are among the many choices awaiting visitors to this destination.

TRANSFORMERS
THE RIDE

S.E.A. AQUARIUM

This is one of the world's largest aquariums with more than 100,000 marine animals across 800 species on display. It is also home to 200 sharks and visitors can learn more about these predators of the sea.

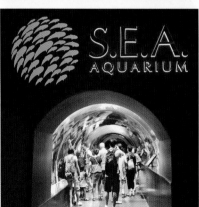

ADVENTURE COVE
WATERPARK

This aquatic adventure park boasts
six thrilling water slides. The more
adventurous can feel the adrenaline
rush as they ride Southeast Asia's
first hydro-magnetic coaster. Those
who prefer something easier can
chill out at the Bluwater Bay wave
pool. Guests can also snorkel over
a colourful coral reef with 20,000
friendly fish.

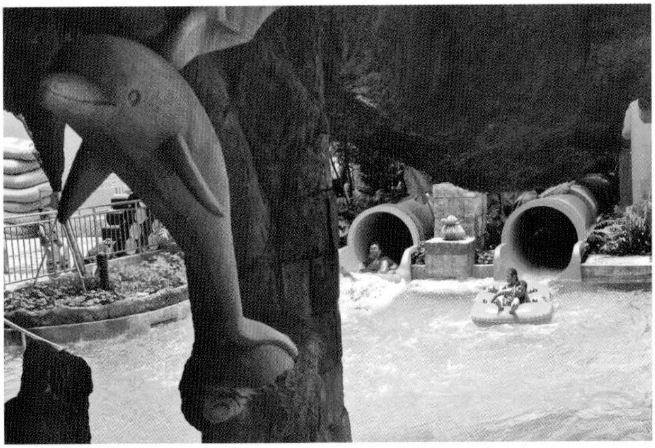

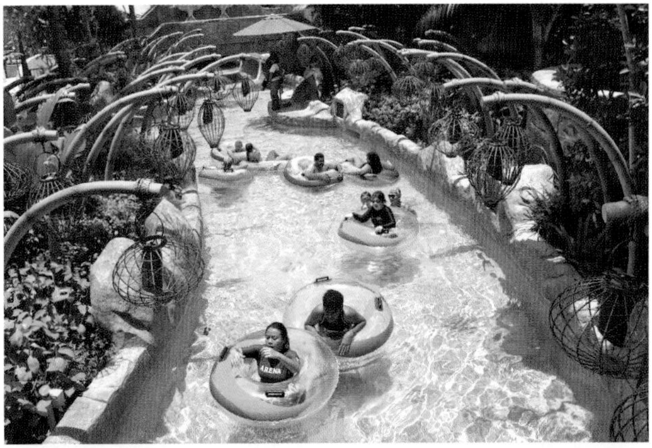
ARENA

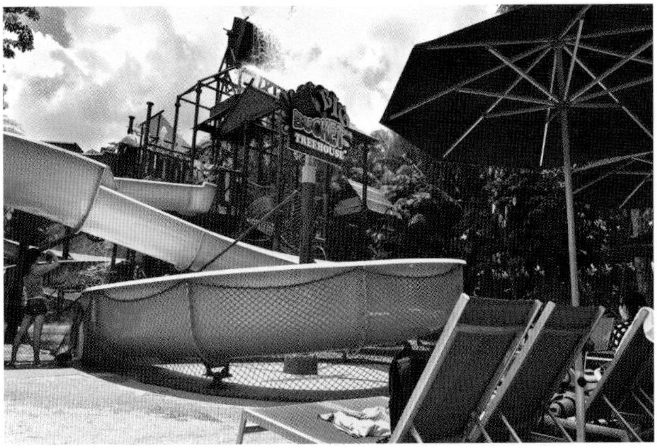
TREEHOUSE

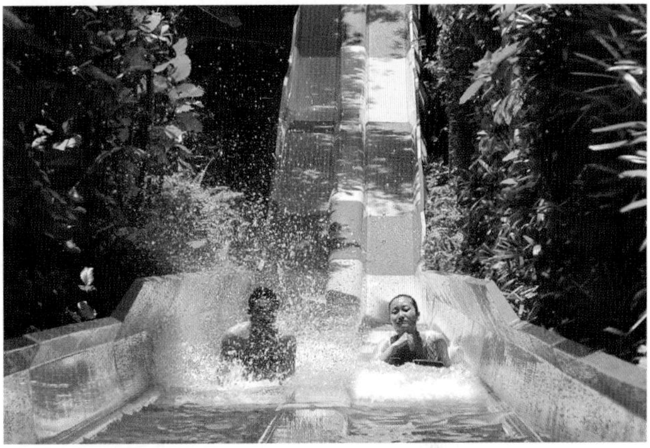

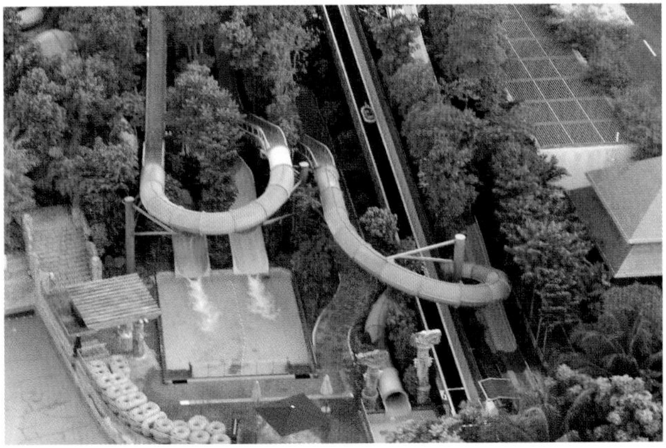

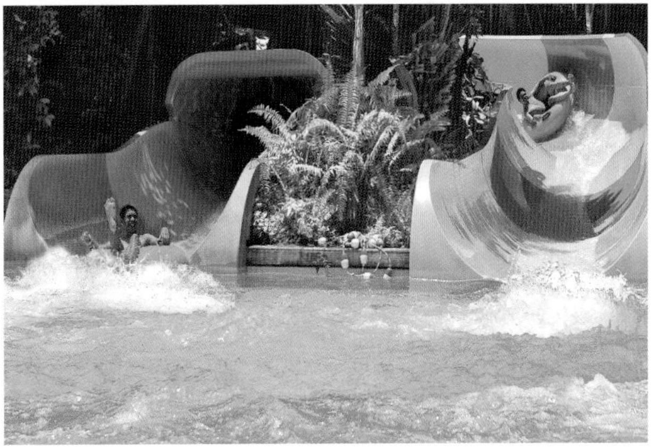

MARINA BAY SANDS

This architectural marvel has redefined Singapore's skyline, the landmark Marina Bay Sands Integrated Resort offers everything from a luxury hotel to state-of-the-art convention facilities, as well as an eclectic mix of retail boutiques and restaurants by celebrity chefs such as Daniel Boulud, Mario Batali and Tetsuya Wakuda. Taking pride of place at the top of the hotel towers is the Sands SkyPark, a sky oasis featuring lush greenery, gourmet dining options and an infinity pool overlooking the central business district.

SINGAPORE FLYER

Strategically located in the heart of bustling Marina Bay, the 165-metre tall Singapore Flyer — the world's largest giant observation wheel — offers an amazing 360-degree panoramic view of Singapore.

SINGAPORE AIRLINES FORMULA 1
SINGAPORE GRAND PRIX

Adrenaline aficionados and glamour fashionistas alike look forward to each September, when the world's only Formula 1 night race takes place at the transformed Marina Bay Street Circuit. The annual event ramps up the glamour, bright lights and high-octane action from renowned Formula 1 drivers the likes of Fernando Alonso, Sebastian Vettel and Lewis Hamilton.

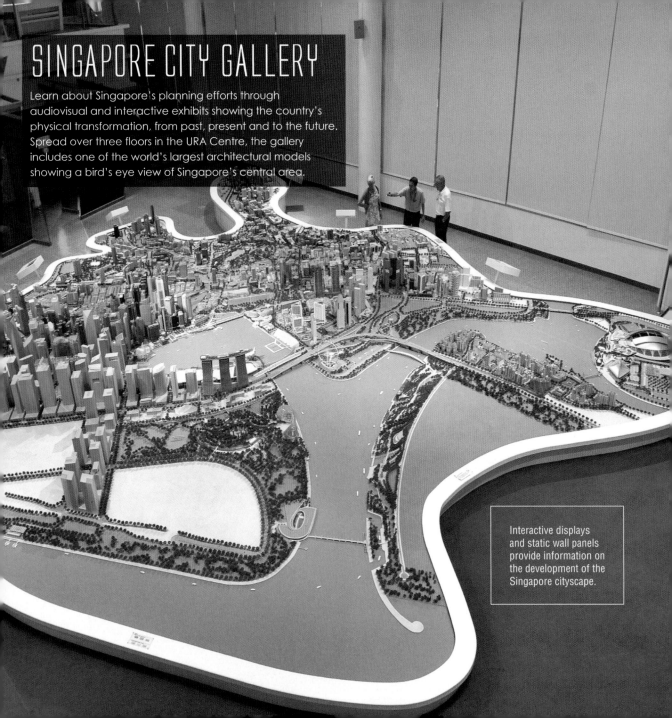

SINGAPORE CITY GALLERY

Learn about Singapore's planning efforts through audiovisual and interactive exhibits showing the country's physical transformation, from past, present and to the future. Spread over three floors in the URA Centre, the gallery includes one of the world's largest architectural models showing a bird's eye view of Singapore's central area.

Interactive displays and static wall panels provide information on the development of the Singapore cityscape.

SINGAPORE ZOO

Over 2,800 animals make their home at the Singapore Zoo, an open-concept rainforest zoo with spacious surroundings akin to their natural habitats. Marvel at the elephants of Asia and catch playful orang utans in the world's first free-ranging habitat, or have breakfast with the gentle primates at the award-winning "Jungle Breakfast with Wildlife" programme.

The polar bear, Inuka, is part of the Frozen Tundra exhibit which features an ice cave with a waterfall and a pool filled with giant icebergs.

NIGHT SAFARI

As night falls, the day has just begun for over 2,500 nocturnal animals at the Night Safari. Embark on a fascinating journey through the world's first open-air wildlife night park, and spot animals such as lions, clouded leopards and Indian rhinoceroses as they frolic and graze by the moonlight.

RIVER SAFARI

The River Safari is Asia's only river-themed wildlife park. It is inspired by the world's most iconic rivers: the Mississippi, Congo, Nile, Ganges, Amazon, Mekong and Yangtze. Housing one of the world's largest collections of freshwater fauna, River Safari features over 6,000 animals including 40 threatened species.

GIANT PANDA FOREST

The main attraction at the River Safari is the Giana Panda Forest. This climate-controlled biodome is the home of giant pandas Kai Kai and Jia Jia as well as the red pandas and elegant golden pheasants.

JURONG BIRD PARK

The largest bird park in Asia, the Jurong Bird Park is a haven for more than 5,000 feathered friends from over 400 species. Watch as majestic hawks, falcons and eagles perform stunning aerial manoeuvres in a simulated hunt in the popular Kings of the Skies Show, and get up close and personal with over 600 free-flying birds in the world's largest walk-in Waterfall Aviary.

ABOUT THE PHOTOGRAPHER

Bernard Go works in the creative industry and is a photo enthusiast. He spends much of his free time capturing images of what he sees around him; finding inspiration in street scenes, good food, well-designed items and exceptional architecture. He is also the photographer behind *Images of Gardens by the Bay*.